MW01109337

# Fall Garden Planning

## Create a fall planting calendar for your Southern vegetable garden: a "how to" guide

### By Amy Whitney

Small Garden News
for your organic garden
from the Southern U.S.

## Acknowledgements

I am grateful for the encouragement provided by many individuals, including family members Joe, Zack, and Jake Dirnberger and Sarah McNamara, and for friends who have helped along the way, including Renae Lemon, Cheryl Stiles, Jo-Evelyn Morris, Ken Johnson, Susan Dawsey, and Steve and Cherie Miller.

This booklet is dedicated to all the Southern gardeners who have puzzled over what veggies to plant and when to plant them for the fall garden and not found a reliable answer.

SAFFRON CROCUS, A FLOWERING BULB FOR THE UPPER SOUTH, BLOOMS IN FALL AND IS THE SOURCE OF CULINARY SAFFRON.

# Contents

# Dear Gardener,

When I first started growing vegetables in Georgia, my fall plantings were not a resounding success. It took a few years before I worked out which crops to plant for a fall garden and when to plant them.

Now, after a busy season of tending, watering, and weeding the summer garden, I look forward to the slower pace of a productive fall garden. The cool weather of fall and early winter reduces the frequency of tasks like watering and weeding, and there is less of a rush to harvest. The vegetables will hold a little longer in the garden before passing into the over-mature stage.

With a fall garden, I can rest, while still bringing good food to the table. If your Southern fall garden in the past has not produced as well as you had hoped, this little guide is for you.

This fall garden planning guide provides information about the selection of crops, setting a planting schedule, and getting the soil ready for the crops you have chosen.

This book is not intended as a general guide to vegetable gardening, and some topics are touched on only as needed to make adjustment for the fall garden.

Gardeners in other regions might also find helpful information here, but the intention is to support gardeners in the

Southeastern U.S., in plant hardiness zones 7, 8, and 9, from the Carolinas and across to East Texas.

The results of research and the experiences that helped my fall garden be more successful are in this booklet. My hope is that other Southern gardeners can benefit, too.

Best wishes for great gardening,

-Amy Whitney

CABBAGES IN LATE SEPTEMBER IN AUTHOR'S NORTH GEORGIA GARDEN.

# What Goes into a Fall Garden?

Most of the crops we plant in summer can't get through a frost without some damage, like wilted or burnt leaves and fruits. These summer crops, such as tomatoes, peppers, cucumbers, squashes, and okra, are called warm-season crops. They are not the ones that will survive — and thrive — through the frosts and freezes of fall and early winter.

To get food from the Southern garden through November and beyond, the garden needs to be replanted in late summer with cool-season crops. These crops produce vegetables in the cooler weather of fall, winter (in the Southeastern U.S., at least), and early spring.

We call them cool-season crops, but most will need to be planted while the weather is still warm. Finding space in a summer garden that still is producing good food can be a trick. Having a plan that allows for a range of planting dates for different crops will help make your fall garden a success.

'BLUE CURLED KALE' STANDS UP TO LIGHT FROSTS WITH NO SIGNS OF INJURY.

# What are the cool-season crops?

Gardeners can choose from a wide selection of crops for a fall garden. Here is a list of some, though not all, of the cool-season crops that do well in a fall garden in much of the Southern U.S.:

| | |
|---|---|
| Beets | Lettuce |
| Bok Choy (Pak Choi) | Mustard greens |
| Broccoli | Onions, bulb type |
| Brussels sprouts | Onions, bunching |
| Cabbage | Parsley |
| Carrots | Radishes, salad |
| Cauliflower | Radishes, winter |
| Cilantro | Rutabagas |
| Collard greens | Shallots |
| Garlic | Spinach |
| Kale | Swiss chard |
| Kohlrabi | Turnips |

For the most part, if the crop is a fruit or vegetable that has seeds inside, it probably is not a cool-season crop. You can see that the list of fall crops is heavy on leafy greens, root crops, and vegetables in the cabbage family. Broccoli, bok choy, cabbage, Brussels sprouts, cauliflower, collard greens, kale, kohlrabi, mustards, radishes, rutabagas, and turnips are all cabbage-family plants.

Some gardeners are surprised to learn that winter squash is not on the list of fall garden vegetables. After all, it has the word "winter" right there in its name! In reality, we plant winter squashes — butternut is one example — in late spring, to grow and mature in the heat of summer.

For these squashes, the word "winter" refers to the keeping quality of the harvested vegetable. They do not need to be canned or frozen for use in winter; the squash keeps just fine in its unprocessed form for a few months. Some varieties actually become sweeter several weeks after harvest.

SALAD GREENS (AND WEEDS) IN A NOVEMBER GARDEN.

# When Do We Start Planting?

This is the weird part. For some of the cool-season crops, the best way to make sure the plants have plenty of time to mature may be to get them into the ground — or started in flats— in the middle of August!

I learned this the hard way. My first few tries, I planted crops that didn't make it through the winter, or that didn't reach full size until sometime in spring, before I really figured out how to make a planting schedule.

Maybe you are a more laid-back gardener than I am and are not really concerned with harvesting greens and beets in the fall, as long as you get to harvest them eventually. If that is the case, then you can start your fall planting a little later, maybe even three or four weeks later, than a schedule like mine would call for. In the Southern U.S., you will likely still bring in a harvest from the later-planted crops; it might just be in spring instead of fall.

Other gardeners, like me, will want to keep good food from the garden coming into the kitchen as many days each year as possible. For those gardeners, the planting schedule should be pretty tight.

# How to Find Planting Dates

We have more than one option in creating a planting schedule. The first is the most simple; just use the general planting date ranges listed on seed packets. The other method, based on specific days-to-maturity for the exact variety of a crop that you have chosen, will take a little more work. It is the method, though, that has brought the most success to my fall garden. Both methods are described below.

## Planting date ranges on seed packets

Many seed packets show a range of planting dates for the crop inside. Not all packets have this information, so you may need to do some research in catalogs or online to find planting-date recommendations for the varieties you've chosen.

The recommendations often show broad ranges, like "July-August". If that is the planting range on your seed packet and you live in the lower South, you would choose a date in late August. If you live in the upper South, you might select a date in mid-August. The July dates in this example are for Northern gardens.

You can use the planting-date ranges to create a basic planting chart for your fall vegetable garden. Just get out your calendar and make a note in the right time-frame for each crop you are going to plant. That is super-easy, and it works well-enough for many crops.

If you have tried this first method of determining when to plant, and your fall crops have not matured when you thought they should, you might want to try a more targeted method of finding a planting date.

This second, targeted method is based on counting back the number of days-to-maturity for each variety from an estimated frost date,. This is the method that has given me my most successful fall gardens, and it is explained next.

# Counting back from a first frost date

This method starts with finding an estimated first fall frost date for your yard. For my yard, a reasonable estimate for a first frost date is around November 1 in most years. The first frost is sometimes a couple of weeks later, and sometimes it is a few weeks earlier.

How can you identify a reasonable frost date for your yard? If you live in Georgia, you can use information from University of Georgia's automated weather stations (weather.uga.edu), like I did. These stations are in locations all over the state, and the data are posted online.

Searching the weather data online showed me how variable our first frost date can be. Over a 15-year span, the first autumn frost at my nearest couple of weather stations ranged from October 19 (2009) to November 15 (2015, 2004). Going farther back, to the year 2000, there was a frost recorded at the weather station in Dallas, GA, on October 10. However, in many years the first frost occurs within a few days of November 1, which is how I chose that date.

If there isn't a weather monitoring station in your area, you can get an estimate for a frost date from your county's Cooperative Extension office. These offices operate all across the U.S.

After determining an estimated first frost date for your yard, you can use that as a starting point, to count back days-to-maturity and find a planting date for each variety of your crops. The backs of most seed packets include the days-to-maturity information, and some seed catalogs may include that information for the varieties that they offer.

Why do I look for a separate planting date for each variety? All lettuces do not reach full size in the same length of time, and neither do all beets, or all varieties of any crop. Days-to-maturity for varieties of kohlrabi vary from about 45 days for 'Kolibri' to 58 days for 'Early White Vienna' to 130 days for 'Gigante'. Identifying different planting dates for each variety allows the right amount of time for each one to reach maturity.

The cool-season crops will continue to grow beyond that first frost date, but growth will slow as the weather becomes more consistently cold. Planting the fall crops early enough that they reach harvest-size soon after the first frost means that we can harvest full-sized vegetables in early winter.

Fall crops that are planted late might be too small to survive an early hard freeze. If they do survive, they might not reach maturity until sometime in spring. Using the counting-back method with a reasonable first frost date improves the odds of planting not-too-early and not-too-late.

# Create Your Own Planting Schedule

This is how to create a planting schedule for your fall garden based on your own frost date and the days-to-maturity information for your seed varieties:

- Identify an acceptable estimate for the first frost date for your yard.

- Locate the days-to-maturity information for your seed varieties on the backs of seed packets or in a seed catalog.

- Count back that number of days (or convert days to weeks, for easier counting) from the frost date, adding one more week to account for slower growing as the weather cools.

# An example of how this works:

I have identified a reasonable first frost date for my yard of November 1. I have a packet of 'Witloof' chicory seeds that says the plants need seventy days to reach maturity. This information is sometimes also called "days to harvest". Seventy days is ten weeks.

For cool season crops, that days-to-maturity number is based on speed of growth in the spring. For fall gardens, we add one more week to that number, to adjust for slower growth as the weather cools. This gives me a planting date, for 'Witloof' chicory, of eleven weeks in advance of November 1.

I use an old-time print calendar to find the date that is eleven weeks before November 1, and I land on the date August 16. In other words, I find November 1, see that it is on a Thursday (in another year it may be on another day of the week), and then I count back eleven Thursdays.

If that exact day turns out to be too busy or rainy for getting seeds into the ground, I try to get the seeds planted as close as I can to that date. This is a schedule for seed-planting in my yard, **using a November 1 frost date**:

A blank chart, formatted like the one in the example below, is on the last pages of this book. It is for you to use in creating your own planting schedule.

| Days-to-maturity | Weeks before frost (days to maturity plus one week) to plant | Approximate planting date |
|---|---|---|
| **35 days** | 6 weeks | September 20 |
| **42 days** | 7 weeks | September 13 |
| **49 days** | 8 weeks | September 6 |
| **56 days** | 9 weeks | August 30 |
| **63 days** | 10 weeks | August 23 |
| **70 days** | 11 weeks | August 16 |

Note: If the days-to-maturity number for your seeds does not exactly match a number on the chart, add it to the row that is the closest match.

For the chart to make sense, read across the center of the book.

| SEEDS to plant around this date | TRANSPLANTS to plant around this date |
|---|---|
| Salad-type radishes | Cauliflower |
| Salad-type radishes, 'Tom Thumb' lettuce, 'Bloomsdale' spinach | |
| 'Red Russian' kale, 'Buttercrunch' lettuce, 'Perpetual spinach' Swiss chard, 'German Giant' radishes | Broccoli or cabbage |
| 'Detroit dark red' beets, 'Marvel of 4 seasons' lettuce, cilantro | |
| 'Lacinato' kale | |
| 'Witloof' chicory, 'Nantes' carrots, 'Watermelon' winter radish, 'Georgia' collards | |

# Isn't it too hot outside?

Some cool-season crops are very sensitive to hot weather. Lettuces will turn bitter and "bolt" if they are in the garden while it is too hot. When we say bolt, we mean that the plants will send up a stalk for flowers and then go to seed.

When plants switch over into flowering, they quit putting out new, tender, tasty leaves. This is a good reason to choose varieties that have a relatively short days-to-maturity. You can plant them after the hottest part of summer, reducing the risk of bolting.

Broccoli, cauliflower, and Brussels sprouts are also very sensitive to heat. In the South, we set those crops into the garden as plants, also called transplants, instead of as seeds. Plants can go into the garden much later, when the worst of the summer heat has passed.

Even when planting is delayed by choosing to set out transplants rather than seeds, the weather can still be too hot; cool-season plants may become scalded in the afternoon sun. Providing shade for the first several days after planting your transplants can reduce heat-stress on newly planted crops.

Salad radishes are oddballs in that they do not make a good crop in the summer heat, but they also can't stand a hard frost. My family has an extreme fondness for radishes, and the short season for these used to be a major frustration. Basically, I can get in two or three successive plantings in fall and another two or three in spring, but that is it. Since salad radishes do not keep well in storage after harvest, our radish season is short.

At least, it was short until I started planting winter radishes, which can stand colder weather. Winter radishes are turnip-sized, and they need to be planted in my garden in late August and early September. They can take seventy or more days to reach full size. Harvest, for me, begins in mid-to-late November.

A WINTER RADISH, 'MUNCHENER BIER', HARVESTED IN DECEMBER.

# Your yard's microclimate

My North Georgia yard is at a low point in the neighborhood, bordered on one side by a little creek. It tends to be slightly cooler than the nearest weather stations, and it can have slightly different frost dates.

Some years my yard has frost when yards further up the hill do not. My yard's microclimate — the slight difference due to where it sits in the neighborhood — is something that I take into consideration when planning the garden.

Knowing that my yard can have a slightly earlier frost helps me know that I can be a few days earlier in planting fall vegetables, and a few days later with my spring and summer crops, than many of my neighborhood gardening friends.

As a result, when a planting day on my chart is going to be inconvenient for planting, I try to get the work done a few days in advance of my scheduled planting-day instead of a few days later.

If your yard is a little warmer, maybe because your garden is on a warm, South-facing slope, then you might decide to plant a few days later than your scheduled day. If your garden is cooler, like mine, then knowing that can help you plan your planting schedule for improved productivity.

# Exceptions

Some gardeners include a section of "baby greens" in the garden. These are cool-season greens that we harvest while the plants are small instead of waiting for them to be fully grown. You can plant these through most of the spring, summer, and fall, and harvest multiple times. Some packets of Mesclun mix and other mixed greens/salads are designed with this kind of planting and early harvest in mind.

Gardeners can make two or three cuttings from each sowing of seeds. To keep a continuous supply, make a fresh planting every couple of weeks.

# Should I Choose Seeds or Little Plants?

Seeds are usually the least-expensive option. Many cool-season crops do well when seeds are planted right into the garden. This assumes that there is room in your garden to plant seeds for your new crops.

If your summer garden is still full of healthy, productive plants late into the summer, buying plants may be a good choice for many fall crops. The plants, also called transplants, can be set into the garden much later than seeds, as much as six to eight weeks later. This gives you more time to harvest any remaining summer crops.

YOUNG PAK CHOY PLANTS GROWN FROM SEED IN THE GARDEN.

For some crops, like carrots, buying plants or starting plants in pots is not practical, because they do not transplant well into the garden. If you have only a little space cleared in the garden at planting time, you might want to use some of it for carrots.

[Note: I did try to transplant carrots once, that I had started from seeds in a deep tray. They were very hard to transplant, trying to keep the roots straight, and the resulting mature carrots were bent, forked, and weird. In a way, the experiment worked, but the carrots were super-hard to clean and cut up to use in cooking.]

If you are going to rely on cool-season vegetable plants from your local garden center, buy them as soon as they appear on the shelves. Then, plant them as soon as you can. Plants that have not had time to become root-bound in their pots as they sit around for weeks on end will be more productive!

Another option is to grow your own transplants. You can start plants from seeds in flats or pots, using the same planting dates you set on your own planting schedule. The plants may experience a brief slowdown in growth when you transplant them into the garden, as they work to repair root-damage that occurs at transplanting time. Recovery is usually quick, though; this should not make too big a difference in when your crops start producing enough leaves, or big-enough roots, for you to harvest.

For all crops, choosing varieties with shorter days-to-maturity lets you plant a little later, keeping the cool-season plants out of the summer heat.

The table below shows which crops are most commonly planted as seeds, which are set out as little plants, and which are planted as "other" (bulbs, cloves, sets).

| CROP: | PLANT THIS: |
| --- | --- |
| Beets | Seeds |
| Bok Choy (Pak Choi) | Seeds |
| Broccoli | Plants |
| Brussels sprouts | Plants |
| Cabbage | Plants |
| Carrots | Seeds |
| Cauliflower | Plants |
| Cilantro | Seeds or plants |
| Collard greens | Seeds or plants |
| Garlic | Cloves |
| Kale | Seeds or plants |
| Kohlrabi | Seeds or plants |
| Leaf Lettuce | Seeds or plants |
| Mustard greens | Seeds |
| Onion | Sets or plants |
| Parsley | Seeds or plants |
| Radish (all types) | Seeds |
| Shallots | Bulbs |
| Spinach | Seeds |
| Swiss chard | Seeds |
| Turnips | Seeds |

# Extending the Harvest

Cool-season crops vary in their cold-hardiness. Most can take temperatures down into the mid-twenties without any damage. Many can stand up to even colder temperatures. Spinach has been the most cold-hardy of all my cool-season plantings. Leaves might be a bit damaged, but the plants survive to regrow after nights down below ten degrees F. Other gardeners have told me that Brussels sprouts, a crop I don't grow, are as cold-hardy as spinach.

In winters with less-severe cold snaps, fall-planted broccoli that has already provided one big head keeps on producing more florets (tiny heads of broccoli) down the stem in very-early spring.

Some lettuces, though, and cauliflower, won't survive temperatures down into the low twenties. The harvests from these crops tends to end — in my yard, anyway — in the first really cold weather that comes in mid-to-late December.

You can keep some of the less-hardy vegetables alive and growing if you cover them with plastic sheeting or specially created crop-blanket fabric. The protective covers need to be on supports, high enough that they don't rest on the plants. The covers can be expensive, but they can extend the harvest into January and beyond.

# Before Planting Your Fall Crops

Clearing away summer crops that are no longer producing well is not the only task to complete before planting the fall garden. The remaining steps, though, are not hard or complicated.

## Soil Preparation

The soil still should be in good condition from the work you put into the spring garden. If your garden has heavy clay soil or fast-draining  sandy soil, you probably added a lot of compost and other amendments to help improve the way the soil holds water and nutrients. Some of those amendments added in spring are still in the garden, but it is best to add more every time you plant something.

Composts and other organic-matter-type of soil amendments — rotting leaves and bagged soil conditioners, for example — help the soil in multiple ways. They provide food for beneficial microorganisms that live in the soil. They provide micronutrients that plants need to grow and stay healthy. They improve how water is held in the soil. In heavy clay, they keep the soil from staying too water-logged. In sandy soils they help keep the water from draining away too fast.

In the long, hot summers of the Southern U.S., all that organic matter disappears from the soil pretty quickly. Those beneficial microorganisms break it down. We call the process of breaking that stuff down "decomposition," but the microbes and the other tiny members of their teeming underground world might refer to it as "eating".

This underground activity is why we need to add more composts, ground bark, rotted leaves, and other organic materials to our gardens before we plant our fall crops.

I remember reading, many years ago, in Don Hastings' *Gardening in the South* series of books, about how quickly all those good amendments can disappear. Hastings had one flower bed in particular that he had put some serious effort into improving with composts and other organic-material amendments. It was a very lush and beautiful bed.

He went out of the country and was gone for a few years. When he returned, the soil in that bed had reverted to hard red clay. He had to start all over again to rebuild the health of that garden bed! It is a story that I have never forgotten. It is often in mind as I tend my own garden beds here in North Georgia.

If you are unsure of the minimum amount of compost to add at planting time, aim for a half to one inch layer every time you plant something.

A half inch is about the same as spreading two five-gallon buckets of compost on a four-by-eight foot garden. If you don't have that much compost ready-to-use, a lighter layer of compost can go under a thicker mulch layer (old leaves, straw, or a bagged soil conditioner, not wood chips). The mulch will also help improve the soil as it decomposes. Hopefully, though, you will be able to increase that compost layer to a full inch, or more.

# Fertilizing the Fall Garden

Much of the fertilizer that we spread on our gardens in spring and summer will be gone by now — used up by plants or washed away in rains. More will need to be added to the garden to support our fall crops.

If you sent a sample of your garden soil to a lab for analysis, then you already should have a report that tells how to fertilize your garden. Most states have a soil-testing service offered through their Cooperative Extension offices.

If your soil report says that the soil-nutrient balance and pH (the measure of how acidic or basic the soil is) are close to what your garden needs, that is good news. You can use its fertilizer recommendation for a few years. Sometimes, though, the lab finds that the mineral-nutrient balance and pH are way off target. If that is the case, then you might want to send a soil sample each year until your garden's soil is closer to the mark.

Many gardeners have not sent a sample of their garden's soil to a lab for testing. If you are in that group, you can use an off-the-shelf fertilizer product from a local garden center. Choose one that is for vegetable gardens. Be aware, though, that this will not be individualized to the needs of your own garden.

Labels on fertilizers all will show the amount of the "Big Three" mineral-elements that they contain: nitrogen (N), phosphorus (P), and potassium (K). The information will be displayed as three numerals separated by dashes, looking like this: 2-5-3. The order of the numerals is always the same (N-P-K). The numerals represent percentages. In the above example, a fertilizer labeled with an N-P-K of 2-5-3 contains 2% available nitrogen, 5% available phosphorus, and 3% available potassium. *

How can this information help you? The mineral-elements play different roles in promoting plant growth. I have heard Walter Reeves, also known as The Georgia Gardener, describe the roles of N-P-K in plants as Up-Down-All Around. This means that, in general, nitrogen promotes leafy top-growth (Up), phosphorus promotes root growth (Down), and potassium supports overall metabolic health (All-Around).

If you are buying an off-the-shelf product, remember Up-Down-All Around (leaf, root, and overall health) as you look at the N-P-K ratio on the label. Your leafy-greens may benefit from a product that has a higher nitrogen percentage (the first number), while your root crops may benefit more from a product that has a higher phosphorus percentage (the middle number).

In chemical fertilizers, the nutrient elements are in the form of soluble salts that plants can use right away when they are dissolved in water and are in the root-zone of the plants.

Organic fertilizers have to be broken down by bacteria and other soil-microorganisms first. For fall crops, organic gardeners should add organic fertilizers at, or a few days before, planting time, while the soil is still warm enough for the micro-organisms to be active and the "breaking down" to begin.

Regardless of the kind of fertilizer you choose, be sure to follow the label instructions for how to apply the product, and how much to use, if you do not have specialized instructions from a laboratory soil test.

# Micronutrient considerations

Plants need more mineral-elements than just the Big Three of nitrogen, phosphorus, and potassium. Others are needed in smaller amounts, and some are needed in "micro" amounts. These are the micronutrients. Shortages of any of the nutrients, even the ones needed in tiny amounts, can limit plant growth.

Raised-bed gardens that are filled with commercial growing mixes or any similar compost-peat-and-perlite type of combination are unlikely to have micronutrient shortages. Newer, in-ground gardens might be short on some of the micronutrients.

For example, If you have an in-ground garden in North Georgia, your garden's original soil may be short on boron. The sandy and/or eroded clay soils in this area sometimes are.

Boron is not one of the mineral-elements that spring to mind when we think about fertilizers and plant food, but some crops have a higher need for this micronutrient than others. Broccoli and beets, two of our cool-season crops for fall gardens, are in that higher-need group.

Garden soils in different parts of the South will have their own quirks. Over time, consistent additions of composts and organic-approved sources of plant nutrients, such as kelp meal, will help fill micronutrient gaps in your garden's soil.

# Watering

The reduced water need of the fall garden is one of its great blessings. In the heat of summer, you may have needed to water your garden two, three, or even four days each week for an hour or more at a time. That task is greatly reduced in the cooler weather of the fall garden.

Less water evaporates from the soil, and the plants aren't using as much to keep cooled down.

Even with cooler temperatures, the garden may need to be watered occasionally. For plants to be able to use the nutrients in fertilizers and composts, the soil needs to be kept moist. The soil microbes work much more slowly to break down composts and release nutrients when the soil is dry.

The best way to determine whether your garden needs to be watered is to reach down into the soil to feel with your hands. You are the best moisture-meter there is!  Use a trowel well-away from any roots of your crops to poke a hole into the garden, and reach down several inches. Moist soil does not need to be watered. If it seems dry, then apply some water.

It is also possible to purchase a moisture meter to check your soil's moisture levels. Gardeners who keep house-plants may already have one that they can use in the garden.

# Planning for pests

Organic gardeners try to plan in advance to manage pest problems. In general, pests are less abundant in cool-season gardens, but they can upset our plans of harvesting beautiful, unblemished vegetables.

## Caterpillars

Among the most annoying trouble-makers in Southern fall gardens are the cabbage moth and cabbage white butterfly. The flyers themselves aren't the problem — it is their babies, the caterpillars, that munch away on our cabbage-family plants and leave behind big slimy wads of "frass" (caterpillar poo). The leaves they like to eat are from plants in the cabbage family, which include cabbage, kale, collard greens, broccoli, turnips, rutabagas, Brussels sprouts, and more.

There is an organic-approved treatment for these pests. Any product containing Bt for caterpillars (a bacterial-derived product) will do the trick, but I would rather not apply any pesticide, even an organic one, when I can avoid it. A better answer for a small garden is to cover the plants with small-meshed netting. The netting keeps the flyers from laying eggs on the plants.

The same system of support that you will use to protect your garden from extreme cold, covered with spun crop-blankets or plastic, can be used to hold netting up over the garden.

You can use bird netting, and tulle from a fabric store also works. Be sure to pin the edges down to the soil. Those moths and butterflies are trickier than you might think; they will find any big-enough gap in your defense system.

If your garden has a different pest problem that appears every year, plan a way to manage the problem before planting.

CABBAGE-FAMILY PLANTS UNDER NETTING, PROTECTED FROM EGG-LAYING CABBAGE BUTTERFLIES AND MOTHS.

# Aphids

Another common pest in fall gardens is the aphid. Actually, it can be aphids (plural) in crowds of what seems like tens of thousands all on one plant. These little, soft-bodied insects can be attracted to leafy crops like lettuces and kale.

Sometimes, aphids are attracted to crops that have been given enough nitrogen fertilizer (the mineral-element that pushes leafy-green growth — remember?) that the leaves are extra-delicious. If your greens have aphids, the first step is to think back about your fertilizer. If you used a little extra nitrogen to support leafy-green growth, you might refrain from adding any additional nitrogen to plants in the infested area until the aphids are gone.

If the infestation is not too severe, you can smash them by wiping the leaves with your fingers. If that is too disturbing for you, wiping with a cloth will also work.

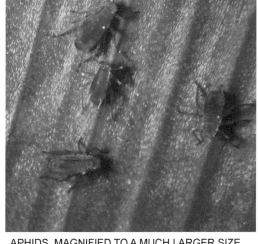

APHIDS, MAGNIFIED TO A MUCH LARGER SIZE THAN YOU WILL EVER SEE ON YOUR PLANTS.

The next step is to wait a few days to see if any aphid-predators show up. In organic gardening, knowing that there are predators like parasitic wasps provides an odd kind of comfort. Parasitic wasps inject their eggs inside aphids, and the wasp babies, after hatching, eat the aphids from the inside. Ladybugs and green lacewings are other very effective predators on aphids.

In my own garden, waiting for the insect-predators is often all I need to do to clear up an aphid problem.

Unfortunately, though, sometimes an infestation is so extreme that even large swarms of ladybugs plus any nearby parasitic wasps and/or lacewings are not enough to wipe out the aphids.

If your local predators leave too may aphids behind, the next suggestion is to blast your sturdier plants with a strong spray from a hose to knock the aphids off. Aphids are not good navigators; neither are they good climbers. Once they are knocked off, most will not be able to find their way back to your leafy greens.

Your next option is to try an insecticidal soap spray. In a dire emergency, try a garden pest spray that contains Neem. Of course, the very first thing to have done, if your experience is that aphids come to your greens every year, would have been to cover the sure-to-be-afflicted crops with a spun row-cover soon after planting, to keep the aphids out completely.

## Root-knot Nematodes

These tiny, soil-dwelling pests can interfere with the condition and productivity of your crops. You won't see them in a shovelful of dug-up soil, even if you look very carefully. If you have plants that are not growing or producing well, that might even be looking a little sickly, the best and fastest indicator that these pests are causing the problem is the appearance of a crop's roots.

Checking the roots involves pulling up a plant, which can be a hard task for a gardener. However, roots of infested plants will have a knotty appearance. The root galls (the knotty-looking parts) that form from the activity of the nematodes make it harder for nutrients and water to move up to the leaves and stems.

Even though I know that my garden soil harbors these pests, I manage to get plenty of food by using some specific strategies. The first thing to know, though, is that managing a root-knot nematode infestation is a year-round project.

One important strategy is to try to keep up with the weeding. These nematode pests can grow and multiply inside the roots of many common weeds, and, of course, the growth of the weeds does not seem to be not hindered at all!

Root-knot nematodes tend to cause more trouble in rainy, warm years. They don't grow and multiply well in cold or in drier soils. This is lucky for our fall crops, because for much of the winter, while soil temperatures are below about 60 degrees F, the nematodes will not be active.

You can put that information into action by turning the soil on a dry, cold day. This strategy exposes root-knot nematodes to conditions that are unfavorable. This can reduce their numbers in garden soil.

Normally, I would not recommend frequent soil-turning, but if a garden is heavily infested, then the situation could be considered an emergency. In that case, turning the soil on more than one dry, cold day, if the weather cooperates, would be a good idea.

Another strategy to implement is to plant collard and mustard greens as a solid cover crop. Their presence can suppress

'GREX' BEET WITH KNOTTY ROOTS, FROM ROOT-KNOT NEMATODE INFESTATION.

root-knot nematode populations. A week or two before planting the next round of crops in that space, turn under those greens, to let them decompose in the garden, to get the most benefit.

Root-knot nematodes do not attack all crops, which is very good news. In the fall garden, root vegetables are commonly affected crops. The enlarged roots can become misshapen by damage from these pests.

For crops that are susceptible, even in other seasons, I choose varieties that are labeled as being resistant to root-knot nematodes when possible. The labeling does not mean that the crops will not be attacked, but it does mean that they can grow and produce in spite of an attack.

Research shows that resistant plants can actually reduce the numbers of root-knot nematodes in their patch of soil. That means that this strategy is important for warm season crops, like tomatoes, as a way to keep the nematode population under control through the summer. This is part of the "year-round" aspect of root-knot nematode control.

Another "year-round" strategy is to plant a cover crop, closely-spaced, of marigolds that can reduce populations of root-knot nematodes. Some marigolds actually attract these pests, so look for varieties like 'Nema-Gone' and the French marigolds such as 'Tangerine' that are known to work as root-knot nematode population reducers.

These strategies, and more not listed here, will not make the nematodes go away. They can, though, keep the level low enough that our garden plants are healthy and productive, even when root-knot nematodes are present.

# Fall Crops for Southern Gardens

Public research universities in each state study crop varieties and make lists of those that do well in their state. Among the Southeastern states, there is good agreement about which varieties stand up to our weather and soil conditions. From those lists, I have pulled names of recommended varieties for fall gardens across the Southeast, to include in this book.

Along with the selected recommended varieties in this section are notes about either care, common pests, disease issues, or other useful information. Planting depth information given is for seeds. Spacing recommendations show a range that reflects the range of sizes of varieties within the crop.

An established days-to-maturity for each variety included in this section is in parentheses following the variety name. You may find that your seed packets give slightly different numbers than are found here. In my research, I found that different sources did not always agree on the days-to-maturity for every variety.

Days-to-maturity given for broccoli, Brussels sprouts, cabbage, and cauliflower reflect the time after setting transplants into the garden. If you choose to grow these from seeds, indoors, add about 40 days to the listed days-to-maturity. In other words, start them indoors about six weeks earlier than when you plan to put the plants into the garden. For many of us, this means starting seeds for these crops in July, or even June.

# The Crops

## Beets

Detroit Dark Red (60 days), Red Ace (50), Kestral (53), Cylindra (60), Golden Detroit (55), and Little Ball (50) are among our reliable varieties. The leaves are good to eat, along with the roots.

Each beet seed is actually a cluster of three or four seeds. The beets will grow larger if you thin them when the seedlings are about three inches high.

Beets do not compete well with weeds, which means their part of the garden needs to be kept as weed-free as the gardener can manage. Beets also need a fairly loose soil to allow their roots to get large. Heavy clay soils will need amending with soil conditioners and composts to be made beet-friendly.

Planting Depth: 0.5 to 0.75 inch
Plant Spacing: 4-5 inches

## Bok Choy (a.k.a. Pac Choy, Bok Choi)

Joi-Choi (50 days), Ching-Chiang (50), Shuko (45), and Mei Qing Choi (45) are among our recommended varieties. This crop grows best in cool, moist soil. These are cabbage-family plants, which means the same pests that afflict broccoli and cabbage, for example, can cause trouble for these plants. Grow them under netting to prevent cabbage butterflies and moths from laying eggs on them. The caterpillars that hatch from those eggs will ruin these plants.

This crop stands up well to frost and light freezes, down to around 28 degrees F, but in a hard freeze, this crop will suffer, so plan to harvest and eat these plants when they reach mature size. You can create a staggered harvest of this vegetable by planting more than one variety, making sure to plant two or three that reach maturity at different times.

PAK CHOY IN THE GARDEN.

These plants send up a flower stalk and set seed rapidly in warm weather, making this crop a better choice for the fall garden than the spring garden.

Planting Depth: 0.5 inch
Plant Spacing: 4-10 inches

## Broccoli

Arcadia (63 days), Packman (64), Premium Crop (65), Waltham (74), Southern Comet (55), and DiCicco (49-78) are among the recommended varieties for the South. The days-to-maturity for this crop reflect the time it takes to reach harvest stage after setting transplants into the garden.

After the  main head of tightly closed buds forms at the top of the plant, harvest by cutting below where the branching for that head begins.

If you leave that main head of broccoli in the garden too long, the tiny buds will expand and then open into yellow, four-petaled flowers. It will be beautiful, but probably not the vegetable you were hoping for.

Heads of broccoli will be damaged by a freeze. If very cold weather (below about 28 degrees F) is predicted, harvest all the good-looking heads to avoid losing the crop.

After harvesting the main head of broccoli, you can leave the plants in the garden. If the weather does not get too cold, the plants will make more, small "heads", also called florets, down the main stem. Packman in particular produces a lot of those mini side-heads.

Premium Crop is a larger plant that makes a very large main head, but it produces fewer mini side-heads.

This is a cabbage-family plant, so watch out for caterpillars.

BROCCOLI, READY FOR HARVEST.

Plant Spacing: 12-20 inches

# Brussels sprouts

Jade Cross (85-100), Long Island Improved (80-115), and Royal Marvel (85-100) are recommended varieties for the Southeastern states. A little round sprout forms at the base of each leaf up the main stem. If the weather is warm while the sprouts are forming, they will make loose clumps of leaves instead of firm sprouts. This tendency means that Brussels sprouts will be more reliable as a fall crop than as a spring crop in the South.

Harvest the sprouts when they are about an inch across. Pulling off the "companion leaf" when harvesting each sprout makes the process easier.

If your Brussels sprouts never seem to make a crop, even after a few years of trying, consider testing your soil for boron. This crop has a higher need for boron than some others. However, do not be tempted to add boron without a soil test result. Once added to the soil, boron cannot be removed, and too much can harm other plants.

Aphids and caterpillars are among the pests that eat these plants.

Planting Depth: 0.25 inch
Plant Spacing: 18 inches

# Cabbage

Blue Vantage (72 days), Bravo (85), Stonehead (67), Rio Verde (85), Red Acre (76), Early Jersey Wakefield (64), Round Dutch (75) are some of our recommended varieties.

Cabbages are frost tolerant, but outer leaves will be damaged in a hard freeze, and the whole plant can turn to mush in extreme cold (down below around 22 degrees F). Caterpillars can make an awful mess of this crop, so be sure to grow it under netting.

If you select a non-hybrid type, like Round Dutch, individual plants will reach maturity at different times. This creates a staggered harvest that many home-gardeners prefer.

You will know that a head of cabbage is mature when it is tight and firm. A soft head is a sign that the vegetable is not yet ready for harvest.

Plant Spacing: 12-18 inches

# Carrots

Varieties for the South include Danvers 126 (75 days), Chantenay (75), Thumbelina (50-75), Purple Haze (70), Nantes (65-75), and Apache (65). Seeds can take as long as two weeks to germinate.

Carrots do best in raised beds or looser soils. If your garden soil is fairly stiff with clay, try Thumbelina, which is more round than long. I have grown Little Finger (55-60), a small

FEATHERY LEAVES ABOVE GROUND SHOW WHERE THE CARROTS ARE.

variety that isn't on the Southern vegetable variety lists I've seen, with good success in my in-ground, red-clay garden.

To determine whether your carrots are large enough to harvest, reach down to the base of the leaves to feel for the "shoulders" at the top of the root. Each variety will be a different size at maturity, so check your seed packet or catalog description to find out how large yours should be at harvest time.

Root-knot nematodes can cause misshapen and forked roots.

Planting Depth: 0.25 inch
Plant Spacing: 3-4 inches

# Cauliflower

Snow Crown (70 days), Candid Charm (95), Freedom (66), and Snowball (80) are recommended varieties for the South.

This crop can be finicky. The plants are fairly cold hardy, but the mature heads should all be harvested in advance of a hard freeze. To keep the heads white, pin or tie the leaves over the head after it is two to three inches across, to keep the sun off. You can save yourself the work of pinning up the leaves by planting a self-blanching variety, like Snowball, whose leaves naturally hug the top of the growing head.

Snowball forms a larger head than some varieties, and it forms best as a fall crop since this variety is day-length sensitive. If you plan to grow cauliflower in both fall and spring, choose Snowball for fall and a different variety for your spring crop.

Plant Spacing: 15-18 inches

LEAVES OF A YOUNG 'EARLY SNOWBALL' CAULIFLOWER CURL AROUND THE HEAD, PROTECTING IT FROM THE SUN.

# Cilantro

Choose any variety. This cool-season herb will bolt in warm weather, making it an easy choice for the fall garden, when warm weather is less common. Most years, plants will continue to grow slowly through the winter, then begin more rapid growth as spring progresses. You can harvest leaves beginning when the plants are about six inches tall and continue until the plants die. I start planting these six to eight weeks before the first frost.

Planting Depth: 0.5 inch
Plant Spacing: 12-18 inches

# Collard greens

Most varieties do well all across the South, including Vates (68 days), Morris Improved Heading (70), Georgia Green (80), Champion (75), and Top Bunch (70).

The leaf disease Downy Mildew can cause yellow-turning-brown spots on the leaves. I have seen this disease in larger gardens in North Georgia. If you suspect that your collards have Downy Mildew, switch to the variety Morris Improved Heading next year; it has shown resistance to at least one strain of this disease. Also, try to keep the leaves dry when you water the garden. This mildew thrives in cool, damp conditions.

Georgia Green does especially well in the sandier soils that underlay many Southern gardens.

Aphids and the caterpillars of cabbage butterflies and cabbage moths sometimes become a problem on these plants.

Planting Depth: 0.5 inch
Plant Spacing: 12-16 inches

# Garlic

Choose either a Creole, Italian, or Silverskin type. Our best harvests typically are from these soft-neck garlics. Hard-neck garlics produce a hardened stalk with a curled "scape" (flower-and-seed head) at the top. Soft-neck garlics don't. Soft-necks are also the kind commonly sold in grocery stores, which is where many gardeners find a garlic bulb to pull apart for planting.

GARLIC GROWING IN THE WINTER GARDEN.

Plant individual cloves, still in their papery wrappings, as early as two-to-four weeks before the first frost. Push them root-end-down into prepared garden soil three to five inches apart, with the pointy-tip about one inch below the surface of the ground. These will grow all winter long. Heads will form underground as the days lengthen and warm in spring.

If you miss planting before the frost, you can still plant later in winter. The shorter time in the ground means that the mature garlic bulbs will be smaller than if you had planted at that earlier time, but you will still get garlic bulbs.

When about half of the leaves have turned from green to brown and yellow, it is time to harvest the garlic. This will be sometime in early summer. In my North Georgia garden, this happens in mid-June most years.

After harvest, let the garlic cure in a single layer in an open area, until the bulbs are dry, for a few weeks before using. I lay mine on the covered front porch.

This curing makes them easier to peel and lengthens their storage-life. Clean the bulbs and trim the roots off before storing your crop in a dry, well-ventilated area.

The milder flavored Elephant garlic can also be grown. It is a type of leek rather than a true garlic, but you can treat it like a garlic in the garden. Be sure, though, to leave more space between cloves at planting time, to allow room for the larger bulbs to grow.

Planting Depth: So that the tip of the clove is about 1 inch below the soil surface
Plant Spacing: 4-5 inches

# Kale

Vates Dwarf Blue Curled (55 days), Tuscan (Lacinato) (60), Winterbor (60), Dwarf Siberian (50), and Red Russian (50) are among our recommended varieties. This is another cabbage-family plant, with the potential for caterpillar and aphid attacks.

RED RUSSIAN KALE.

Kale is a great choice for a fall garden since frost can improve the flavor. If the winter is not too cold (below ~15 degrees F), most kale will live through the winter and produce more leaves in early spring. Winterbor survives the coldest winter temperatures for gardeners in my area.

The Tuscan, Red Russian, and "bor" types can grow to be three feet across by late spring. If your garden is small, try the Dwarf Blue Curled. Harvest outer leaves as the plants grow, but do not harvest more than a third of the plant at one time.

Planting Depth: 0.25 to 0.5 inch
Plant Spacing: 8-18 inches

# Kohlrabi

Recommended varieties include Early Purple Vienna (60 days), Winner (45), Early White Vienna (55), and Grand Duke (50).

I used to think of this as a "California vegetable", and not a crop for the South, until we grew some at a community garden where I volunteered. These were easy to grow and delicious! Harvest when the enlarged stems — the part that looks like an above-ground bulb — are two to three inches in diameter. Very little of this plant goes to waste, because the leaves are edible, too. Keep the garden bed moist to reduce the odds that the fat stems become woody.

This is another cabbage family crop.

Planting Depth: 0.5 inch
Plant Spacing: 4-6 inches

# Lettuce

We have recommendations for three main categories of lettuces:

<u>Romaine</u> - Cimarron Red (65 days), Flashy Trout Back (55), Green Towers (74), Parris Island Cos (65), Outredgeous (64)

<u>Leaf</u> - Sierra (54), Red Sails (45), Black-Seeded Simpson (49), various Oak Leaf types (45-60)

<u>Head</u> - Buttercrunch (55 days), Esmerelda (48), Maverick, Tom Thumb (48), Ermosa (52)

Root systems of lettuces are small and shallow. This makes them a great crop for container-growing. It also means that they

may need to be watered more frequently than other crops. Keeping the plants watered and fertilized will help them to continue growing well. If the plants dry out, the leaves can develop a bitter flavor.

LEAF LETTUCE, THE OAK LEAF VARIETY BRONZE ARROW.

The most cold-hardy of the three main categories are the leaf lettuces, and for me the Oakleaf types, such as Bronze Arrow and Green Oakleaf, have been the cold-weather champions, surviving lower temperatures than other varieties.

Seedlings can become dried out in a strong wind. If your garden is in a windy location, placing loose pine-straw around the seedlings can support the tender, young plants and reduce wind damage.

If you are looking for a Southern "native," try Parris Island Cos, which was developed in a collaboration of Clemson University and the USDA.

Planting Depth: 0.125 inch, or right on the damp soil surface
Plant Spacing: 6-12 inches

# Mustard greens

Southern Giant Curled (45 days), Tendergreen, Green Wave, Florida Broadleaf, and Red Giant (43) are among the recommendations for Mustard greens in the South.

This is another crop that is likely to bolt (send up a flower stalk) in warm weather, making it a good choice for the fall garden. You can harvest by cutting the whole plant, cutting leaves off a couple of inches above where they branch out from the stem, or just cutting outer leaves a few at a time.

Planting Depth: 0.5 inch
Plant Spacing: 6-10 inches

# Onions, Bulbing

Southern Belle, White Candy, Savannah Sweet, and Granex 33 are recommended varieties. (All take several months to mature, and will be ready to harvest in late spring or early summer.)

Bulbing onions for the fall garden should be planted as onion sets (tiny dry bulbs), and they need to be short day-length varieties like those listed above. Long day-length varieties will not form bulbs reliably in the South.

Plant onion sets a few weeks before the estimated first frost date, at the earliest.

Onions have shallow root systems. If the soil gets too dry, growth of your onion crop can slow down, resulting in smaller bulbs at harvest. They are considered "heavy feeders", which means they will benefit from a little extra fertilizer as the weather warms in spring, and they do best in fairly loose soil.

Some bulbs may send up a flower stalk before the leaves have died back enough for harvest. These onions do not keep well or long.

Any bulbs that send up a flower stalk should be used in the kitchen as soon as possible after harvest, so they won't just rot and go to waste.

Onions are ready to harvest when the tops of most of the crop have fallen over, with leaves turning tan or brown. After harvest, set the onions in a dry, shaded place for a week or two to cure. After the

BULBING ONIONS SET OUT TO CURE AFTER HARVEST.

outer layer (the skin) has dried, trim off the roots and leaves before moving your onions to a longer-term storage area.

If you miss the fall planting window for bulbing onions, you have another opportunity in late winter, but at that time the onions should be planted as green transplants. They will be in garden centers as rubber-banded bundles of baby-onions.

Planting Depth: Plant dry sets, root-side down, so that the pointed tips are about one inch below the soil surface.
Plant Spacing: 4-5 inches

# Onions, Bunching

Evergreen (60-120 days), Parade (65-120), and White Lisbon Bunching (60-120) are recommended. Plant these as seeds in the fall, to harvest green onions in spring. These onions do not form bulbs, but they do multiply. The bunches can be divided when you need green onions for the kitchen, with some being left in the garden to continue growing and multiplying.

The long range of days-to-harvest given for each variety reflects two separate goals. The shorter time shows how long it takes until green onions are large enough to pull and use in the kitchen. The longer time shows how long it takes for the onions to be mature enough to multiply into bunches.

Planting Depth: 0.25 inch
Plant Spacing: 3 inches

# Parsley

No specific varieties are recommended; all are good. This herb-and-salad-green is grown through the winter in much of the South; I start new parsley in fall to grow through the winter in my North Georgia garden and in container plantings. Parsley can keep growing through the following summer, providing leaves for salads and other dishes over a long season.

Some patience may be required as we wait for the seeds to germinate. It can take as long as two-to-four weeks after planting before the seedlings appear.

Planting Depth: 0.25 inch
Plant Spacing: 6-18 inches

# Radish, salad

Lists of recommended varieties for the South include standards like Cherry Belle (24 days), White Icicle (29), Sparkler (24), French Breakfast (26), and Champion (28), but I have successfully grown many more varieties in my north Georgia garden. They all grow best in cool, moist conditions, and should be harvested as soon as they reach mature size. If left too long in the garden, they become hotter in flavor and woodier in texture.

Leaf pests that bother other cabbage family plants — caterpillars and aphids in particular — can bother radish leaves, but radishes often are left alone even when other related plants nearby are being attacked. Cutworms sometimes feed on the outer layer of the root, leaving scrape marks.

Planting Depth: 0.5 inch
Plant Spacing: 2-3 inches

## Radish, winter

Try all of them: Daikon types (50-60 days), Misato Rose (60), Watermelon (60), Munchener Bier (55), Black Spanish (53), and more. Roots of most of these enlarge during times of shortening day length, so they produce their turnip-sized roots only when grown as a fall crop.

RADISHES FROM THE NOVEMBER GARDEN.

They will make leaves as a spring crop, but not the enlarged roots. At my house, we slice these thinly using a mandolin, then sprinkle the slices lightly with salt to enjoy as a light snack.

Planting Depth: 0.5 inch
Plant Spacing: 3-5 inches

## Rutabagas

American Purple Top (90 days), Long Island Improved (80-115), Laurentian (90), and Champion Purple Top (80) are recommended. This crop is similar to turnips, but the more-elongated roots need additional time to reach maturity. The leaves can be eaten, too.

This classic winter vegetable stands up to frosts and mild freezes and stores well in cold storage conditions. People often serve this vegetable mashed with white potatoes in a 50-50 mix. When they do, it pretty much tastes like rutabagas.

Root-knot nematodes, if present, can deform the roots.

<u>Planting Depth:</u> 0.5 inch
<u>Plant Spacing:</u> 6 inches

# Shallots

Louisiana Evergreen, Matador, and Prisma are recommended varieties. (Like garlic and bulbing onions, they grow over several months, reaching maturity in early summer.)

These grow best when planted in fall, several weeks before the estimated date of the first frost. Each individual shallot that you plant will grow to form a cluster of shallots.

When the leaves have died back in late spring or early summer (mid-June in my North Georgia garden), dig up the clusters of bulbs. Some of them will already be visible on top of the ground. That is fine.

Like for the garlic, which will be ready to harvest at about the same time, leave these in a dry, sheltered place to cure for at least a week before trimming away leaves and roots and putting them into longer-term storage.

<u>Planting Depth:</u> Set bulbs so that the pointed tip (the root-end should be facing downward) is about one inch below the soil surface.
<u>Plant Spacing:</u> 9-12 inches

# Spinach

Winter Bloomsdale (47 days), Melody (43), Tyee (40), and Space (37) are recommended varieties. Harvest outer leaves as they become large. If your spinach is gritty, try growing a smooth-leaf type instead of a savoyed (curled or crinkled) type at your next planting.

Spinach produces best in cool, moist conditions. As the days lengthen and weather warms in late winter, spinach will switch over to flower production. When you see a stem rising up out of the plant, that is a clue that leaf production is about to end and flower production begin. This is your cue to harvest the remaining leaves and pull up the plants, so you can get the space ready for some other crop.

Aphids are a possible insect pest for spinach.

Planting Depth: 0.5 inch
Plant Spacing: 6-12 inches

# Swiss chard

All are good, but recommended varieties include Bright Lights (60 days), Fordhook Giant (50-60), Lucullus (50), Red Ruby (55), and Bright Yellow (57). This crop is related to beets, but it does not make the round edible root. I grow a variety of Swiss chard

SWISS CHARD IN A RAISED BED GARDEN.

called Perpetual Spinach (55).

For all of these, harvest outer leaves as you would for leaf-lettuces. This crop tolerates a mild freeze, but it also works well in the summer garden. If you are short on space for fall-garden greens, consider saving these for spring and summer.

Root knot nematodes can cause problems with this crop. If your plants are attacked by leaf-miners, another possible pest, protect the plants with a row-cover to keep the flying adults from laying eggs on the leaves.

Planting Depth: 0.5 inch
Plant Spacing: 8-12 inches

## Turnips

For a root-crop, look for White Lady (35 days), Purple Top White Globe (50), or Just Right (70). If you are more interested in harvesting leaves, look for Alamo (33), Shogoin (30-70), and Seven Top (45).

When growing turnips for the leaves, not the roots, you can skip thinning the seedlings in the garden. If you are hoping to produce turnip roots, then the seedlings will need to be thinned to make room for the roots to expand.

Shogoin is planted for both leaves and roots, which is why I have included the long range for days-to-maturity. The 30 days is for when you can begin harvesting leaves; the 70 days is for when the roots should be large enough to bring to the kitchen.

Some years, turnips develop black spots inside the roots. This is a possible indication that your soil could be short on boron. To find out, call your local Cooperative Extension office to learn how to get boron levels in the soil tested.

If root-knot nematodes are abundant in your garden's soil, they can deform turnip roots.

Planting Depth: 0.5 inch
Plant Spacing: 4 inches

# If Things Go Wrong

Sometimes, a garden experiences problems that we can prevent. The guidelines presented in this little book are intended to help gardeners avoid many of those.

Sometimes, though, bad things happen to gardens that are well-planned and well-tended, using all the most up-to-date information available. Magnificent gardens all over the world suffer from pounding rains, hail, tornadoes and hurricanes, heart-breaking droughts, plant-eating wildlife, diseases that arrive from above ground and below, exotic insect pests, and other potential hazards. Some things are outside of our control.

If your garden has suffered, remember that each year is new. Each year, we get to start again, making choices that improve the odds of success. We can prepare the soil well, select varieties known to prosper in the South, plant at appropriate times, and watch for insect pests. When all goes well, we eat well, too.

# Ready to plant?

After choosing your crops, making a schedule, refreshing your garden's soil, and considering pest-control options, you will be ready to plant your fall garden.

To help you along the way, I have provided a blank table to use in creating your own schedule. Fuller instructions appear on pages twelve and thirteen in this book, but the summary of steps is repeated here:

- Identify an acceptable estimate for the first frost date for your yard.

- Locate the days-to-maturity information for your seed varieties on the backs of seed packets or in a seed catalog.

- Count back that number of days (or convert days to weeks, for easier counting) from the frost date, adding one more week to account for slower growing as the weather cools.

Your personal planting schedule is on the next page, waiting to be filled in with information for your fall garden.

# Fall Planting Schedule

Estimated First-Frost Date: _____

| Days-to-maturity | Weeks before frost (days-to-maturity plus one week) | Approximate planting date |
|---|---|---|
| **28 Days** | 5 Weeks | |
| **35 Days** | 6 Weeks | |
| **42 Days** | 7 Weeks | |
| **49 Days** | 8 Weeks | |
| **56 Days** | 9 Weeks | |
| **63 Days** | 10 Weeks | |
| **70 Days** | 11 Weeks | |
| **77 Days** | 12 Weeks | |

For the chart to make sense, work across the middle of the book.

| SEEDS to plant around this date | TRANSPLANTS to plant around this date |
|---|---|
|  |  |
|  |  |
|  |  |
|  |  |
|  |  |
|  |  |
|  |  |

# A Final Note

If you still aren't sure that planning a fall garden will be worth your effort, consider this comment from my sister, Sarah, who gardens in Louisiana:

"Fall gardening is my favorite. Tons less work (weeding and watering) and not so much production that a single vegetable eater can't keep up. Yes, there will be some to put up in the freezer, but it's not overwhelming, even with less daylight for harvesting. This all matters for people who have other, during-the-day jobs."

The extra brain-work of counting-back-weeks for each variety may seem unnecessary, when generic planting schedules are easy to find in books and online. However, many of those do not take into account that each variety has its own timeline for reaching maturity.

'Little Finger' carrots mature in 55 days. 'Bolero Nantes' carrots mature in about 70 days. 'Oxheart' carrots mature in 80 to 90 days. They are all carrots, but these are big differences in the time it takes to reach harvest-size. Taking these differences into account in deciding when to plant fall crops can make an equally big difference in whether you can harvest in fall and early winter or have to wait until spring.

Your yard may call for additional adjustments as you create your own schedule, but following the guidelines in this booklet will improve the odds of success for your fall garden.

List your chosen crop varieties and their days-to-maturity on this page, to use in filling out the planting schedule.

CPSIA information can be obtained
at www.ICGtesting.com
Printed in the USA
LVHW070533010520
654828LV00007B/840